Volume 2

RAILWAY PRESERVATION SERIES

Bob Gwynne

CELEBRATION OF RAIL
THE STORY OF RAILFEST

NOSTALGIA ROAD PUBLICATION

The **Railway Preservation** Series™

is produced under licence by

Nostalgia Road Publications Ltd.
Units 5-8, Chancel Place, Shap Road Industrial Estate, Kendal, Cumbria, LA9 6NZ
Tel.+44 (0)1539 738832 - Fax. +44 (0)1539 730075

designed and published by
Trans-Pennine Publishing Ltd.
PO Box 10, Appleby-in-Westmorland, Cumbria, CA16 6FA
Tel.+ 44 (0)17683 51053 - Fax.+44 (0)17683 53558
e-mail:admin@transpenninepublishing.co.uk

and printed by
Kent Valley Colour Printers Ltd.
Kendal, Cumbria +44 (0)1539 741344

© Text: Trans-Pennine Publishing Ltd. 2004
© Photographs: Bob Gwynne or as credited

Front Cover: *Marking its entry into the National Collection, world famous and world travelled 4472* Flying Scotsman *took centre stage in Railfest following a successful appeal to buy it just prior to the event. This book also will play its part in the appeal, with part of the proceeds being donated to future restoration work on 4472.* David Tillotson

Rear Cover Top: *Engines of all sizes and descriptions attended Railfest, including this 15" gauge steam engine built by Cagney Brothers of New Jersey USA.*

Rear Cover Bottom: *The rail show covered the past, present and future of the railway industry, and in some cases this could be demonstrated by one object. The Brush Type-4 (Class 47) diesels were introduced in 1963, and four decades later are still (just) in front line service for companies throughout Britain.*

Title Page: *A typical early-morning scene at Railfest re-creates the atmosphere of a steam shed. From left to right 5972* Olton Hall, *K1 2-6-0 Class 62005 and B12 Class 4-6-0 61572.*

This Page: *In a link to Rocket 150, the* Rocket *replica simmers gently with a replica 1830 Liverpool & Manchester carriage behind. This was one of eight short rides available across the Railfest site on a variety of gauges.*

FOREWORD

Railfest marked the two hundredth anniversary of the moment when the steam engine and the railway came together for the first time, and demonstrated the cheap mechanical transport that would make the industrial revolution possible. It was an event that needed celebrating because, in many ways, it marked the beginning of the world we recognise today. But it was also an opportunity to celebrate both the achievements of today's railway and the immense progress of the railway preservation movement.

This book is a record of that event, and its author, Bob Gwynne was intimately involved in shaping the vision for Railfest and in making it happen.

Above: *The collection of railway vehicles that was assembled at York dominate this book, but the abiding memory of Railfest is as much about people as machines. Here we see 4-4-4 John Terence one of the country's oldest 10¹/₄" gauge engines (built in 1908) playing its part.* National Railway Museum

Railfest worked because people from industry, from heritage railways and from the Museum got together to make it happen and thousands more people enjoyed the result. It was a great success and this is a wonderful record of the nine days in 2004 when as George Hudson said 'mak all t'railways cum to York.'

Andrew Scott
Head of Museum
National Railway Museum

Right: *There were many things to talk about at Railfest, but without doubt the main conversation piece was* Flying Scotsman. *The appeal benefactor Sir Richard Branson arrived at Railfest on the footplate of the engine and helped launch the locomotive at its new home. Even without the spectacle of 4472 steaming into Railfest, the show virtually stopped whilst everyone stood to watch the engine arrive and break a banner marking its official entry into the nation's railway collection.* National Railway Museum

Below: City of Truro, *the first engine to lay claim to 100mph on rails in Britain, passes* Flying Scotsman, *the first engine to have an authenticated 100mph top speed (1934). It is said that the Great Western Railway did not reveal the details of the 1904 run at the time, for fear of alarming a public unused to such high speeds; 100 years later and 100mph by rail is commonplace.* Tony Steadman

RAILFEST: THE INSPIRATION

The British have always had a soft spot for their railways. In 1804 Richard Trevithick's experiment on the Penydarren Plateway in South Wales attracted both the crowds and the commentators. Eight years later the world's first commercially successful steam railway, the Middleton, near Leeds, quickly acquired 50 eager passengers on its first run. When the Stockton & Darlington Railway opened in 1825, Stephenson's *Locomotion* had to cope with its given load and an estimated additional 600 passengers. Four years later the Rainhill Trials near Liverpool proved once and for all that locomotive power was the way forward, and it did so in front of an estimated 10,000-strong crowd.

Above: *With the designer and builder of the* Locomotion *replica Mike Satow in charge and one of the world's oldest surviving carriages (Stockton & Darlington Railway coach 59) in tow, the 150th Anniversary cavalcade of 1975 got off to a memorable start. The original is on display at the Darlington Railway Museum, whilst the replica (built at Springwell Works on the Bowes Railway) is now operated at Beamish Museum; all of which are in County Durham.*
British Transport Films

As the railway age got under way, the 'openings' of new lines were always accompanied by large crowds. Much later, when the State fell out of love with the technology that had provided essential transport for over a century and a quarter, the British public did not.

Top Left: *In 1975, the birth of Britain's first public railway to use steam locomotives from the outset was celebrated at Shildon, using a blueprint established by the London & North Eastern Railway 100 years earlier, namely a cavalcade. Participants are seen at the gathering point, the BR Wagon Works, which finally closed just nine years later. One of the entrants was the prototype High Speed Train, which became the saviour of Britain's non-electrified 'Intercity' network and is still with us today. Interestingly, just a few short months after Railfest, the National Railway Museum opened its new out-station at Shildon, with the official opening taking place on Friday 22nd October 2004.* British Transport Films

Bottom Left: *'Rocket 150' celebrated the world's first inter-city line between Liverpool and Manchester and once again a cavalcade took place. Here BR's last steam engine, Standard Class 9F 2-10-0 92220* Evening Star, *steams past the crowds 12 years after steam finished on BR. This was the last time that a rail celebration closed a main line to ordinary traffic and it seems unlikely that it will ever be repeated. It was also the 'high water mark' of the idea of the 'social railway' just as the values of Thatcher's Britain got into full swing.*

During the 1950s and 1960s, crowds turned out for many of the last trains that accompanied rail closures. The Heritage Railway movement then blossomed into a vibrant volunteer army, which was determined to run for themselves some of these discarded national assets. From painful beginnings they developed into a proficient system of heritage lines and today these groups are in charge of over 380 miles of track and 270 stations.

Between the end of the steam age and Railfest, rail had been nationally celebrated twice, at Shildon in 1975 and at Rainhill in 1980; these being the respective 150th Anniversaries of the Stockton & Darlington and Liverpool & Manchester railways. In addition the long tradition of 'the works open day' continued into the privatised era, although these shows have always been aimed mainly at enthusiasts. The year 2004 marked two centuries of steam locomotion and 100 years of 100mph running, to name but two anniversaries, reason enough for a celebration.

Planning for a major celebration, managed by the National Railway Museum at York, started in 1999. Yet how do you tell the story of the past, present and future of rail in a way that engages <u>all</u> who visit, and not just those with specialist knowledge? Furthermore, how do you have an interesting party for rail at a time when it is regaining its position as a vital part of Britain's infrastructure but is little understood? These were just some of the questions that had to be faced from the outset. This book introduces the ideas and planning that went into Railfest 2004, followed by a photographic portrait of the show itself.

Above: *Rocket 150 in 1980 saw the restoration of the 1837 Liverpool & Manchester 'Luggage Engine'* Lion *(which was also the star of the 1952 Ealing Comedy* The Titfield Thunderbolt)*, by far the oldest working steam engine at that time. Not only did the engine appear in the cavalcade, but it also ran on British Rail metals to Southport and is pictured here near Burscough. However, perceptions of risk have changed greatly over the last 20 years making this kind of scene very unlikely today.* Lion *was saved after C. W. Reed visited Prince's Dock at Liverpool in 1927, where he 'found the ancient locomotive jacked up on blocks, with its driving wheels rattling merrily away driving the dock's pump house.'*

Railfest: Lessons From America

In June 1999 the largest rail show of the 1990s took place at the California State Railroad Museum at Sacramento, California, USA. Part of the sesquicentennial celebrations of California, the event was named Railfair 99. The show was an outstanding success, and despite sweltering temperatures it attracted over 26,000 visitors a day to the half-mile long site. Some of the ideas explicit in the organisation of the show, including theatre performances, film shows and the key role played by volunteers, were incorporated into the planning for Railfest 2004.

Above: *Eureka and Pallisade No 4 of 1875 recreating a cinematic rail scene of the 'Old West' was just one of the tableaux around which Railfair 99 was designed. Many of the ideas explicit at Railfair were incorporated into Railfest.*

Right: *Amongst the 24 steam locomotives and seven diesels plus other historic rolling stock that visitors were able to see at the event, were two 3ft gauge Heisler geared engines from the logging railroads of North America. Here we see a Passumpic Railroad Heisler of 1922 and the Eccles Lumber Co. Heisler of 1915, as they share the turntable; in the background is 4449 'Daylight' (Lima 1941).*

Right: *Railfair 99 saw a number of different approaches to interpretation for the exhibits on the site. Here W. C. Fields and Mae West lookalikes stroll around the site for the benefit of the photographers. This was all part of the presentation and was derived from the influence of railroads on America. In reality the two actors both wrote and starred in the 1940 film* My Little Chickadee, *which also featured a railroad sequence. The practice of using actors, volunteers and paid staff to dress in period costume is fast catching on in the United Kingdom, but getting visitors to dress in similar garb is a little more difficult. The best example of this kind of gathering that really has caught the public's eye is the Goodwood Heritage Revival, which is held at the famous Sussex motor racing circuit each September.*

Left: *Demonstrating the work of the railway past and present was an integral part of Railfair. Here the 'Buckingham Bar Lining Gang' demonstrates how trackwork was done in the days before machines. A great tradition of these gangs are the rhythmic songs they employed whilst track-laying, and which have a strong link with 'blues' music and thus to the genesis of rock and roll. In the background is* De Arend, *a 1939-built replica locomotive from the Netherlands.*

Below: *Railfair 99 featured a mini parade reminiscent of the British cavalcades of 1975 and 1980, this being just possible on the site. One difference was that engines involved ended up outside the show for a brief period. Waiting in the street to be re-admitted to Railfair, and also helping to prove the flexibility of the tradition of an unfenced railway, is the oldest 4-8-4 in existence (Baldwin, 1927). Santa Fe 3751 is owned by the San Bernardino Railroad Historical Society.*

Above: *One of Union Pacific's active steam fleet (844), departs Sacramento with one of the railtours that were associated with the event. Railtours are often a feature of large rail celebrations, yet in California this was such a rare occurrence that the tour had been sold out a year in advance.*

Right: *The railway museum at Sacramento boasts the Sacramento Southern Railroad, a net contributor to the Museum's funds. As a result of this connection, the Museum was able to offer train rides directly from the site during Railfair 99. Here ex-Union Pacific 4466 (Lima 1920) gets ready to haul the next train for the Sacramento Southern Railroad as a 'Docent' (a museum volunteer) explains a point to a visitor.*

Above: *As with Railfair, Railfest had associated railtours. Here* City of Truro *hauls a special railtour to Scarborough at the end of the show on Monday 7th June 2004.*
David Tillotson

Left: *In its guise as* Hogwarts Hall, *5972* Olton Hall *was provided by West Coast Railways to haul the VIP special that launched Railfest. This came about because 4472 was declared a failure at Doncaster during its journey north. It took a great deal of phone calls to get clearance for 5972 to run to York in steam at short notice, showing the cross-industry co-operation on which Railfest was built.*
National Railway Museum

RAILFEST: BUILDING THE SHOW

For a major rail show to succeed in 2004 it was clear that closing an operational railway and running a cavalcade over the route was not possible; even if this could be considered, the removal of ancillary sidings from most railways meant that substantial amounts of new track would be needed for storage and display. As this was out of the question, it was obvious that the celebration needed a site. Furthermore, as the National Railway Museum was to lead the 2004 celebrations, the site needed to be close to its main facility in York (as had been the case with Sacramento and Railfair 99).

Above: *Trackwork sponsors Jarvis start in earnest to prepare the site for Railfest in 2003. The rear vehicle is a road-rail crane and digger, the machine in front is a laser-guided bulldozer, ensuring a level foundation for the new track.*

Fortunately, two derelict railway yards adjacent to the NRM's yard (normally used for the storage of vehicles out of public view) were available. The refurbishment work needed to bring them back to use was to be funded either out of the projected earnings of Railfest, assisted by NRM volunteers, or sponsored by the railway industry. Building the site, complete with 550 yards (500 metres) of new standard gauge track proved no small task.

Top Left: *Preparation for Railfest took more than a year. Here members of the North Yorkshire Moors Railway permanent way gang are seen at work in March 2003 recovering track materials before clearance of the site can begin. They followed a tree-cutting gang that had cleared the site and revealed that the railway formation had almost rotted away.*

Centre Left: *Following the NYMR's clearance gang and with York Minster in the background, work to level the site begins by contractors employed by Jarvis, one of the event's industry sponsors.*

Bottom Left: *Members of the army's 168 Pioneer Regiment Royal Logistic Corps (Volunteers) worked on the show site in late October 2003 to lay the 15" gauge railway. Interestingly, this was the first time since the Liverpool Garden Festival 20 years earlier, that a 15" gauge railway had been laid specifically for a public event.* Tony Steadman

Bottom Right: *It is now November 2003 and the GWR-outline petrol railcar, along with a coach from the Sutton Collection, are used to test out the completed track following a visit from members of the Cleethorpes Coast Light Railway. The CCLR had agreed very early on to be involved with Railfest and they offered rolling stock from the Sutton Miniature Railway that they had acquired in 2002, which had been in store since the SMR closed in 1961.* Tony Steadman

Top Left: *As part of Network Rail's sponsorship of Railfest, they agreed to donate over 550 yards (500 metres) of new sidings plus a new point, and these were laid in March 2004 by Jarvis as part of their contribution.*
Tony Steadman

Top Right: *The Plasser-Theurer designed self-ballaster finishes its run at the NRM in March 2004, having just dropped over 400-tonnes of stone on the new track in under two hours. This machine is by far the largest piece of rail equipment that has ever visited the NRM.*

Centre Right: *Once the track was laid a tamper was brought on to make the job complete during April 2004. On the bay platform (seen on the left of the picture) the curve was too tight for the machine to operate, so this section had to be finished by hand. The crew working on this job were dedicated and cheerful professionals who proved to be efficient track people and turned out to be the kind of workers that the national media might have you believe no longer exist.*

Bottom Right: *When all the work was done the installation looked as if it had always been there. Here Sutton Belle gets ready to depart again on the 15" gauge line whilst the Atlantic & North Western Pullman car Pegasus, originally built in 1951 for the Golden Arrow service, stands resplendent on the adjacent new track.*

RAILFEST: ALONG NARROWER LINES

As railways have used many different gauges, the representation of one of the narrow gauge railways was needed at Railfest if the show was to be a comprehensive celebration of 200 years of rail. Accordingly, the innovative Ffestiniog Railway was invited as they introduced the idea of locomotive power on narrow gauge lines, as well as the powered bogie and the bogie coach, both key elements in today's passenger railways worldwide.

With one of the FR's supporters' groups being local to York, and with advice from the Railway Inspectorate, something new was to be attempted for Railfest. This was to build an operational two-foot gauge railway providing visitors with a genuine sample of the Ffestiniog.

Above: *Pictured with an immaculate-looking* Prince *are some of the team from who made a two-foot gauge passenger-carrying railway at Railfest possible.*
Tony Steadman

Although lacking the Welsh mountain scenery, it was hoped that parallel running with the standard gauge service would provide an alternative attraction. Members of the 'White Rose Group' took up the challenge, with the active support of the FR and Railfest organisers and supported by the NRM's stalwart 'Tuesday Night' volunteer team. The result was a magnificent piece of heritage 2ft gauge line in the heart of Yorkshire. The track itself was originally from the Penrhyn slate quarry's railway and had also once graced the FR mainline.

Top Right: *Track-laying commenced in November 2003 and on the right we see a replica broad gauge third class open carriage, which is awaiting transfer to Didcot following the move of the replica broad gauge engine* Iron Duke. *In turn this allowed a tarmac path to be created around the Railfest site, partly within the rails of the NRM's broad gauge demonstration line; this was important if the show was to have easy access for families and visitors with impaired mobility.* Tony Steadman

Centre Right: *Work continued on the FR two-foot gauge line during the NRM's 'Thomas The Tank Engine' fortnight in February 2004.* Tony Steadman

Bottom Left: *The NRM's 2ft gauge 1937 Ruston Hornsby engine (ex-Naburn sewage works) was pressed into service to complete the new line to FR main line standard.* Tony Steadman

Bottom Right: *Finishing off the job in early May, as the NRM's replica* Rocket *runs by on the standard gauge demonstration line.* Tony Steadman

Top Left: *Dating from 1872, the Ffestiniog's Coach 15 is the world's oldest operational iron-framed bogie passenger vehicle, and it is a surviving ancestor of all modern railway coaches. We see it here on its first ever holiday from Wales, just as it arrives at Railfest early in the morning of 16th May 2004.* Tony Steadman

Middle Left: *In addition to its track duties, the Ruston was put to good use to off-load Coach 15 and the replica 'Curly Roof Van', which had only been finished at the FR's Boston Lodge works two days before.* Tony Steadman

Bottom Left: Prince, *the world's oldest operational narrow-gauge engine (1863), was loaded for transportation with the tender in front of the smokebox, needing careful work with the NRM's forklift truck to get the formation correct and ready for operation. 23rd May 2004.* Tony Steadman

Bottom Right: *A working part of the Ffestiniog Railway at Railfest is seen on the last day of service with* Prince *leading Coach 15 and the 'Curly Roof Van'. Railfest preceded the FR's own special event in September 2004, when the railway preservation society would celebrate its 50th anniversary. Part of those celebrations included* Prince *hauling a train of period stock out of Porthmadog station along the spectacular causeway to the railway's workshops at Boston Lodge.*

RAILFEST: DELIVERING THE EXHIBITS

Getting rail exhibits to the museum is a major problem, given that higher railway speeds and stringent safety precautions often prevent the movement of historic locomotives and stock on the modern rail network. These factors see many preserved locomotives being shipped around the country by road. Yet, access to the NRM site along Leeman Road is prohibited by railway bridge restrictions at either end. Getting all the locomotives on and off the site was to be a logistic nightmare, and this certainly prevented Railfest from having some of the locomotives it would have liked in attendance.

Above: *A fitting exhibit was British Railways Britannia Class 70013* Oliver Cromwell, *which was one of the last engines at the end of the BR steam era. Here it arrives from Bressingham Steam Museum where it had been for 36 years, following the working of the 'Farewell to Steam' 15 Guinea Special on 11th August 1968. The Trinity Rail Group, who are based at the former York Carriage Works, allowed exhibits to be off-loaded at their site ready to be shunted by rail across to Railfest, thus avoiding the 12' 6" low bridge that is the Achilles heel of access to the NRM by road. The 1951 Pacific is to be restored to working order thanks to sponsorship from the readers of* Steam Railway *magazine.*
David Tillotson

Top Left: *The second major exhibit to arrive at the site was E5001, the sole survivor from the Class 71 electric locomotives that had been built for the Southern Region in 1958. This was one of the moves that were assisted by the freight company English Welsh & Scottish Railways, and it was hauled onto the site by 66042* Lafarge Buddon Wood *on 22nd October 2003. The move from Doncaster took at least eight telephone calls to arrange, giving the organisers of Railfest fair warning of the task ahead.*
Tony Steadman

Bottom Left: *Fitting neatly into the Railfest Category 'Modernisation – Successes and Sidelines', the Western Region 'Warships' gave high power for low weight using a German design. It was a Warship Class that was to become Britain's first preserved express diesel locomotive (in the 1970s), but the V200s from which it was derived soldier on in infrastructure service in Europe to this day. The example shown at Railfest, D832* Onslaught, *was restored from scrapyard condition and is now based at the East Lancashire Railway.*

Right: *The exhibits D9009* Alycidon, *84001, 31271 and E27000* Electra *are seen on the East Coast Main Line en-route to Railfest in a move sponsored by GB Railfreight. These locomotives are normally housed at Barrow Hill Railway Centre and were among the few historic exhibits to have the right certification to be moved to the show by rail.* David Tillotson

Left: *A last-minute arrival was the diminutive Darjeeling & Himalayan 'B' class locomotive No. 778 (Sharp Stewart 1889). Withdrawn by the D&H in 1960, the engine went to a railway museum in the USA before being bought and brought back to Britain in 2002. At Railfest, 778 was displayed coupled to a replica D&H carriage, which had been built at the Ffestiniog Railway's works at Boston Lodge.*

Below: *Siemens E4 locomotive of 1909 was one of the surprises of Railfest. Restored to working order thanks to sponsorship and lottery money, the venerable Harton Colliery Electric can move under its own power thanks to a giant battery pack in the accompanying wagon. It is seen being delivered on the evening of 19th May 2004.*

Above:

Here we have a new-build steam engine in the shape of Lyd, a replica of the Lynton & Barnstable locomotive, which is being constructed at the Ffestiniog Railway's Boston Lodge Works. A member of the unloading crew anxiously watches the movement, in order to prevent the mishap of grounding. After it was safely off-loaded, the loco was placed onto the 2ft gauge track that was once part of the internal rail system of the former railway concrete works that formed part of the site.
Tony Steadman

RAILFEST: THE SHOW

One of the biggest issues facing the organisers of any major event open to the public today, is the matter of Health and Safety. This is especially true when the event features live steam in close proximity to the general public. The Railfest day therefore started at 09.30 with a safety briefing to all those working the site.

Locomotive crews in particular were reminded that 'steam engines are oily and hot' and asked to ensure that their visitors, who included many that had never been on an engine in steam before, were made aware of this fact.

Above: *This is perhaps the lull before the storm and a view of Railfest that few members of the public would see. Without a single person in sight, we can enjoy the early morning quiet before the show opened at 10am. It also brings together the unique spectacle of* Blackmoor Vale, Prince, City of Truro *and* Matthew Murray, *four different engines from different parts of the country that would never have normally been seen side by side. Volunteers across the site rose to the challenge of making sure visitors to the 20+ open cabs were made welcome and kept safe. The crews manning the exhibits proved excellent advocates for railways in general and the joys of steam in particular.*

Right: *By way of a contrast, the LNER B12 61572 (built in 1928 to a 1911 design) is pictured with all the atmosphere of a packed yard at Railfest. This is the sole surviving British inside-cylindered 4-6-0, once a common design for passenger locomotives all over the world. Its restoration to working order was a 32-year preservation epic, which included shipping the whole engine to the MaLoWa locomotive works in Kloster Mansfeld, Germany for essential boiler work.*

Below: *The Great Central Railway (LNER O4 Class) 2-8-0 of 1911 represented the 'War Duties' section of Railfest, a neglected side of railway history. Engines like these saw service in various parts of the world during the two world wars, as well as on heavy freight duties, particularly for 'King Coal' in the UK. The last one in commercial use was withdrawn from a colliery railway in Australia during 1971.*
Tony Steadman

Above: *One corner of Railfest moved back to the 1960s, with 84001 the North British Loco Company's final product (and arguably its worst ever), and BR's finest the 9F 92203 (built 1959). The latter was newly outshopped and making its first public outing in steam for a number of years and was also complete with its proud owner, the artist and conservationist David Shepherd, for the first three days of Railfest.*

Left: *Away from the preserved railways, regular use of steam has just about become a distant memory. Organisers of Railfest therefore had to be aware of just how ignorant of steam the public can be, and during the event this glorious array of scalding hot pipe work on 92203 Black Prince had a safety barrier in front of it. Steam locomotive crews were notably careful when operating injectors, without being any less enthusiastic to visitors about their unforgiving machines.*

Right: *Vertical-boilered steam tram* Yvonne, *built in Belgium in 1890, was another Railfest surprise. The exhibit managed to fly the flag for light rail as well as give tribute to the memory of Dr. H. A. Whitcombe who was one of the first 'active' railway enthusiasts. In 1926 Dr. Whitcombe arranged for one of the British Isles' last active steam tram engines to be preserved. This was Northern Counties Committee (NCC) Steam Tram No.1 of the Portstewart Tramway (Kitson 1882), which is now in the 'Streetlife' Museum in Hull.*

Below: *Built in 1949 to an LNER design, the K1 Class 2-6-0 62005 was one of the exhibits that could not stay for the full nine days due to other commitments. It is seen here being lined out, so that having had the finishing touches applied just prior to the show's opening, it would be ready for its dash to the Highlands two days later.* Tony Steadman

Top Left: *In the 1930s the LMS made a bold experiment with diesel-electric shunting engines in an attempt to improve efficiency and reduce costs. These early shunters proved their worth during World War II, and the idea took hold in the post-war era as both diesel shunters and main-line diesel locomotives began to make an appearance. It was therefore fitting to show the 1950s' search for steam replacements with diesel-electric shunter D226 Vulcan, which was on its first visit away from the Keighley & Worth Valley Railway since being preserved there in 1966. The 1956 product of English Electric is a rare surviving prototype from the modernisation era, and it wears a livery similar to that applied to the maker's prototype Deltic locomotive.*

Bottom Left: *Built by Wagen und Maschinenbau in Germany, railbus 79964 was a part of the British Railways Modernisation of the 1950s. About 20 railbuses (of several types) were purchased as it was thought that they offered an ideal solution for maintaining passenger services on lightly-used branch lines. However, the lines these railbuses were designed for did not survive the Beeching era and in 1967 this example also went into preservation at the Keighley & Worth Valley Railway. In Germany hundreds of single railcars were in use on rural branch lines in the 1950s and contemporaries of 79964 (nicknamed 'piglet taxis') have only just gone out of service.*

Top Right: *Of course, Railfest had to cover more than just steam, as the Celebration of Rail was designed to cover the two centuries of railways in Britain. It was therefore essential to have representatives of the 'Change-Over Years', with examples of the diesel locomotives that became a common sight as well as those that did not. One of the successes was the Brush Type-2 diesel as seen here with 31271 (formerly D5677); it was named* Stratford 1840–2001 *at Railfest, in memory of the now-closed locomotive shed in East London. The locomotive was specially re-painted into Trainload Construction livery, thus helping to tell the story of the move away from steam in the 1950s and the pre-privatisation era of BR in 1980s; the latter era dubbed by the organisers as 'Holding the Line'.*

Bottom Right: *Two more products from the era are seen here, as English Electric Type 1/Class 20 D8000 stands in front of Brush Type-4/Class 47 47798* Prince William. *These two engines are now part of the National Collection, as the former Royal Train engine was handed over to the museum during Railfest. The Class 47s were one of the major successes of the Modernisation era. For four decades they have been one of the cornerstones of BR haulage, handling everything from humble freight duties to crack express services. The Class 20s also had a long life on BR, and after they were withdrawn some of the class members were even used on the Channel Tunnel construction scheme.* David Thomas

Left: *The 130-year-old Beattie well tank 30587 was presented coupled to a 'Clay Hood' wagon, and also had the distinction of being manned at Railfest by one of its original crews from BR days. Next to it is one of the historic road vehicles at Railfest, an immaculately presented Bedford 'Green Goddess' built for the Auxiliary Fire Service by the Home Office in 1954 for use in times of civil emergency.*

Below: *This United States Army Transportation Corps 0-6-0T was sent to Britain in 1943 and saw service at Southampton docks before it was acquired by the Southern Railway. In 1968 en-route to the scrapyard, the engine ran a hot axlebox, giving enthusiasts the chance to purchase it for the Kent & East Sussex Railway where it is still based.*

Above: *The birth of today's heavy goods vehicle owes a lot to the London Midland & Scottish Railway, as they developed the 'mechanical horse' during the 1930s. This concept was rapidly expanded by the 'Big Four' and led to BR's huge fleet of three-wheeled and four-wheeled tractor units, along with a massive fleet of articulated trailers. Here a representative selection of these charming vehicles show just how the railways achieved a door-to-door service.*

Right: *In the 1950s the BR Standard locomotives were seen as the shining future of rail transport in Britain, but by 1968 the 999-strong fleet of Standards had been withdrawn and mostly consigned to the scrap. A few stayed operational to the end of steam on BR in August 1968, including 70013 Oliver Cromwell. Sadly, the unique BR Standard 8P 71000 Duke of Gloucester was unable to attend Railfest, due to technical hitches with its latest overhaul.*

Top Left: *The Middleton Railway near Leeds holds a unique place in history, as it was the world's first railway to be authorised by an Act of Parliament. It was also a major pioneering line in the early days of steam locomotives, as Matthew Murray and John Blenkinsop pioneered a rack and pinion system of operating the line. Today it is preserved as an industrial railway, and one of its engines a Manning Wardle 0-6-0T of 1903 gained unexpected glory at Railfest. Named* Matthew Murray *in honour of the original locomotive pioneer, this little contractors' engine, which actually helped build one of the GWR main lines, took over from one of its more illustrious counterparts when it deputised for* City of Truro *from Monday to Wednesday on the standard gauge ride.*

Bottom Left: *The oldest steamable locomotive in the country, Furness Railway 20 of 1863, is one of several lottery rebirths. The way it survived after being discarded by the Furness Railway was coincidentally something of a lottery as well. Following just seven years service on the railways around the southern part of the Lake District, the engine was sold to Barrow steelworks in 1870 and re-built as a saddle tank engine. Thankfully it subsequently 'survived' to the point where it was given for public display, albeit used as a children's climbing frame rather than a museum exhibit. The engine was restored to its original condition and returned to steam (with open cab and tender) in 1999.*

Top Right: *Speed has been a huge pre-occupation of the railways during the 20th century, with the long routes north to Scotland being the major battlegrounds between the LMS and the LNER. On the East Coast route, the stars of this era were the Gresley Pacifics, such as* Mallard *and* Flying Scotsman. *Today these survivors are a big attraction at any railway event, but in addition to those two famous engines now resident in York, visitors found an unexpected bonus at Railfest! Like a guest in a hurry, A4 Pacific 60009* Union of South Africa *(built at Doncaster in 1937) arrived late for the party and left early, hauling a York to Newcastle excursion on June 5th. However, those who saw it, either in York or out on the main line, had an additional reward. Here it is steaming below the electric overhead wires at Beningbrough, as it hurries past one of the historic signs that have been preserved on the East Coast Main Line.* David Tillotson

Bottom Right: *Another symbol of the fast East Coast route were the English Electric 'Deltic' locomotives, of which just 22 production examples and one prototype were built. The prototype and D9002 are in the National Collection, but the museum was glad to welcome D9009* Alycidon *in its 'as built' livery. It provided Railfest visitors with a startling contrast to the 15" gauge terminus station adjacent to it. Also seen at Railfest was the cab of another Deltic, 55008* Green Howards, *which was saved for preservation in 1982.*

RAILFEST: PEOPLE

Loco-owning groups were asked to keep their carefully selected engines open to the public throughout Railfest, and the preservation world rose to this challenge as volunteers from all over the country descended on York. These ambassadors for the story of Britain's railways spent their days at Railfest answering questions ranging from the astute to the downright funny, but they did so with one common denominator – their love of rail.

Above: *The ex-LNER B12 Class 4-6-0 and its crew pose for the camera, yet 61572 has now been in preservation longer than it actually spent in railway service. Designed by Holden of the Great Eastern Railway in 1911, the B12s were re-built and substantially improved by Nigel Gresley in 1932. They were casualties of the early dieselisation of East Anglia and were scrapped in the early-1960s. However, given its epic restoration story, the crew of 61572 can perhaps be forgiven for looking pleased with themselves.*
Tony Steadman

Above: *Here a crew member exhibits a bit of tender loving care on* Blackmoor Vale, *which is dressed in its finest Southern Railway livery and numbering. As one of the first 'footplate' experiences that visitors to Railfest encountered when reaching the display area, the team were kept busy for nine days explaining Southern lore; covering everything from rat's tails to the Golden Arrow.* National Railway Museum

Right: *Visitors looking at the footplate crew of the Middleton Railway's* Matthew Murray *could not fail to observe the broad smiles that were evident. The 1901-built engine was pressed into passenger service for three days to substitute for the 1903-built* City of Truro, *which needed minor firebox repairs during Railfest.*

Above: *People of all ages gained memorable experiences from Railfest, and the public in particular loved the access to cabs in steam. This picture captures the kind of scene that happened at Railfest, which was all about creating positive memories of rail, giving the technology its rightful place in a developing Britain. Such interchanges are essential if we are to demonstrate the railways of old to future generations.*
National Railway Museum

Left: *All dressed up with nowhere to go, but with plenty of time to stop and chat! In their period clothes, the 'Heritage' crew from Furness Railway No.20 proved that talk was one of the winning ingredients at Railfest.*
Tony Steadman

Right: *As steam railways owe their origins to the genius of Camborne-based Richard Trevithick, it was appropriate for his early inventions to be represented at Railfest. A crew-member of the replica of Trevithick's Camborne road engine of 1801 swaps notes with a crew-member of the Beattie well tank. The road engine was one of the forerunners of the Cornish engineer's locomotive designs, which of course would lead to the creation of the Penydarren locomotive of 1804. The crew of the 1801 replica reckon their engine is good for 17mph, but thankfully for the event's insurers there was no space to test this assertion at Railfest. The Beattie well tanks would also later become synonymous with Cornwall, where they eked out their final days on branch trains and china clay workings.*

Below: *Newly outshopped but not yet in steamable condition, the 1925 vintage 30777* Sir Lamiel, *another product of the North British company (like 7754 and 84001), represented the 1920s and 1930s. This was of course the era when steam was unchallenged on the crack expresses of Britain, and part of a long-gone golden age. Here the crew pose together on the last day of Railfest.* Tony Steadman

Above: *Former Great Western Railway pannier tank 7754, built by the North British Loco Co, was specially returned to the National Coal Board (NCB) livery in which it retired in 1975. This was the last ex-BR steam engine to be operated in ordinary commercial service, albeit with the NCB, but thereafter it became another epic of preservation. When the Llangollen Railway first got the engine, a member reported that 'everything that could possibly be bent, was'; it took a full 17 years to restore it to working order. But it was another sign of the times, as some Railfest visitors were heard to ask 'what does NCB mean?'* National Railway Museum

Left: *In 1992 a volunteer at Llangollen is seen at work restoring 7754, even though it was a complete engine and not a hulk from the Barry dump. All the historic rail exhibits at Railfest were the result of hard work by volunteers who have achieved the near-impossible over the years, often with limited resources.*

Above: *Beer, coal and steam, just one of the combinations for visitors to enjoy at York. The USATC 0-6-0ST* Wainwright *was parked adjacent to one of the coal bunkers at Railfest, which itself was not far from another great British tradition – beer. The result was one of the unique drinking experiences of 2004, made all the more atmospheric by* Wainwright's *need to get to over 100psi in order for its injectors to work.* Tony Steadman

Right: *Another Southern Region survivor was the Beattie 2-4-0WT, which was built by the London & South Western Railway in 1863. On board this engine, one of just two survivors from an 85-strong class, a crew member cooks his breakfast in the traditional way. This demonstrates one of the reasons why a French reporter described Railfest as being 'a feast for the senses, having colours and sounds, as well as the smells of coal, oil, sausages and boiled onions'.* National Railway Museum

Saved for the Nation

From the start of the planning for Railfest, *Flying Scotsman* had been a 'must have, if at all possible', so early approaches were made to the company that operated it. However, no firm arrangements had been made right up to the time that rumours appeared in the railway press and wider media about the locomotive being for sale in February 2004. By this point in time, the dream of an Edinburgh home for the engine was over and the NRM's management took the decision that York was where the engine should be, if only the money could be raised to buy it!

Above: *Whilst the crowds gathered, a last-minute clean was needed for 4472* Flying Scotsman *before the world's most famous steam locomotive joined the National Collection!* Tony Steadman

Although the NRM's small Sponsorship team were deeply committed to raising funds to ensure Railfest happened, it now required an additional effort to secure 4472 for the nation. Despite the extra work a public appeal was launched and with media support the mammoth total of £3.2 million was raised. This included around £365,000 from over 6,000 private donors, a figure which was matched pound-for-pound by Sir Richard Branson.

The public response to the appeal prompted the National Heritage Memorial Fund to give a grant of £1.8 million, and by the end of March it was clear that the engine was going to join the National Collection. In addition Yorkshire Forward gave a grant of half-a-million pounds to help with the interpretation of this national icon. The success of the appeal was overwhelming and culminated with Sir Richard Branson riding into the event on the engine's footplate. This was of course a highlight of Railfest and really was the day that the 'People's Engine' came home!

Top Right: *A hero's welcome was given to* Flying Scotsman, *which has been in the public eye since it entered service in 1923. It shares the name of the express from London to Edinburgh that has run since 1862, and as a result many people feel they know the engine, even though they have never seen it. Hence, everyone at Railfest on Saturday 29th May wanted to see the official hand-over of the locomotive as it passed into the care of the National Railway Museum.* Tony Steadman

Bottom Right: *So great was the reception for 4472, that trains on the 15" gauge line had to stop for a couple of hours until the crowds died down. The 'People's Engine' was soon open for all to see, and here the public get their chance to visit the cab, waiting in a queue that did not die down for nine days.*

THE MODERN ARENA
@ RAILFEST

The railway industry of today contributed hugely to the comprehensive nature of Railfest, as they provided exhibits of all kinds that were manned by staff from all over the country on a specially prepared site. Exhibits were chosen to show that rail has a vibrant future in Britain and the area was easily as busy as that given over to the steam exhibits. GNER even provided a travel enquiry desk, which was kept busy throughout the event.

Above: *Representing the old era, but still operating after over four decades of service, the Class 47s are only just coming to the end of their operating lives. Here in a two-tone green livery, D1748* Abertawe Landore *is in the Modern Arena.* Tony Steadman

Right: *Also just ending their service lives are the Class 56s, and 56006 was a late addition to the show. Specially repainted in 'Rail Blue', this import from behind the then 'Iron Curtain' was built in Craiova, Romania in 1976 and represented the 'Holding the Line' era of BR.* National Railway Museum

Top Right: *Built in London (Ontario), the Class 66 locomotives mark the move away from freight trains hauled by diesel locomotives derived from the Modernisation Plan of the 1950s. Today there are more than 300 of these in traffic in Britain and here we see 66200 paired with BRA steel wagon 964046.* National Railway Museum

Centre Right: *Speed of service has become one of the significant ways in which rail has developed over recent years, and engines such as 67015 look to have an exciting future in Britain. The Class 67 locomotives are capable of 125mph running, hence it was appropriate for a class member to be at Railfest. Members of this class are kept as 'Thunderbirds' or rescue locomotives for fast services such as those provided by GNER, and two of them have now replaced the Class 47s as Royal Train engines.* David Thomas

Bottom Right: *Representing the most up-to-date approach to infrastructure maintenance, Jarvis-owned Plasser & Theurer 09–3X tamper liner graced the Modern Arena. The track foundations of the high-speed railway that we enjoy today are created by these machines, the first of which came into use in 1947. Named* Peter White *(DR73110), this piece of plant was a rare opportunity for visitors to see just how high-tech our railways have become. Jarvis also provided demonstrations of the 'Slinger' tracklaying train.* National Railway Museum

Above: *'It's still got its chalk marks!', commented one visitor upon viewing Southern Class 171 Turbostar DMU, which was brand new from makers Bombardier in Derby. Seen in the new Southern livery of franchise South Central, the Turbostar is the most successful of the post-privatisation diesel units and represents the future of passenger travel on many lines in the UK. The Modern Arena @ Railfest was co-ordinated by the Railway Forum and situated on a site completely derelict six months prior to the show; it proved as popular to visitors as the 'Heritage' displays.* National Railway Museum

Left: *Railfest aimed to show the past, present and future of rail, providing contrasts between modern railways and the survivors of a bygone age. Although there are opportunities to see modern trains alongside those from heritage railways at various places around the country, Railfest gave a unique opportunity to draw up some really fascinating contrasts; take for example this view of a brand new Pendolino train seen through the spectacle plate of the Furness Railway's No.20.*

Right: *The Virgin Pendolino 390043* Virgin Explorer *was of great interest to Railfest visitors. This modern tilting train is one of the new units that have been designed to slash journey times on the West Coast Main Line. Yet we could have had this technology many years before, and to prove it the Pendolino was parked within sight of the APT(E) prototype tilting train, which British Rail retired in 1976.*

Below: *To mark ten years since the Channel Tunnel opened, Eurostar 3313* Entente Cordiale *was invited to Railfest. Although it was in Paris on the Tuesday before the show began, Britain's rail speed record holder (205mph 334.7km/h in July 2003) arrived in time (behind 67015) and then became another star of the show.* National Railway Museum

RAILFEST: OPERATIONS

A major theme of Railfest was the operation of trains, and not merely having locomotives and rolling stock on static display. The NRM's existing tracks at the back end of the site were considerably extended in advance of the event, and this provided the opportunity to have trains moving around the show, thus giving emphasis to those displays that remained stationary. The general impression that visitors gained was that there was always something moving around them, creating sights, sounds and smells that a static display could never hope to achieve.

Above: *Here we have the little and large of Railfest, as the Sherwood Forest Railway's 15" gauge* Smokey Joe *passes Sir William Stanier's 6233* Duchess of Sutherland. *The ex-LMS Pacific was at Railfest until Friday 5th June when it left for a railtour. Built in Crewe in 1938, the 4-6-2 locomotive is one of several steam engines that were originally preserved as static attractions at Billy Butlin's holiday camps when they were withdrawn from service in the mid-1960s. In recent years the restored 6233 has become a popular engine on railtours and in June 2002, it actually hauled the Royal Train as part of the Queen's Golden Jubilee, the first time for 35 years that this duty had gone to steam locomotive.*

Top Right: *An all-American train on the first 15" gauge railway basks in the unusually fine weather that blessed Railfest on most days. Here Cagney No. 44, which was built in 1910, is seen with a set of Cagney coaches originally from Peru; both are now based at the Rhyl Lakeside Railway, the country's oldest seaside miniature railway. It was trains like those by the Cagney Brothers of New Jersey that prompted the British engineer Bassett-Lowke to have* **Little Giant** *built, to see if he could break into the market for miniature railways. Behind, the Pullman car* Pegasus *(itself the result of a major restoration and rebuilding) and Deltic 9009* Alycidon *complete the scene.*

Bottom Right: Battinson, *a steam-outline diesel engine, was enjoying its first ever days of service since it was built in the 1950s. In front the 99-year-old* **Little Giant,** *drew attention in the paint scheme worn when it started its career (and that of the British 15" 'minimum gauge' genre) at Blackpool in 1905.* Tony Steadman

Demonstrations

In addition to the theme of motion, it was decided to have tableaux that would capture some of the key points in railway history.

One example of this was the heavy horse, Gilbert, which represented the first 200 years of rail history. This horse had also been used to demonstrate horse-shunting at the NRM's earlier 'Railways & Roads' events.

Top Left: *Although horse-haulage of railed vehicles may have very ancient origins, detailed reference to an early railway in Britain dates from 1604 (in Nottinghamshire). This was 200 years before Trevithick's attempt at a transport revolution at the Pen-y-Darren Iron Works. Even after steam entered the equation, horses and railways had a long association, as the railways used them for hauling carriages, wagons and road vehicles. In fact road horses remained in BR service until the mid-1960s and they only retired their last shunting horse 'Charlie' (which was based at Newmarket) as late as 1967. Just visible in the background we see the future of rail Edwardian-style, in the form of Harton Colliery electric No.4.*

Bottom Left: *The true father of the steam locomotive was the celebrated engineer Richard Trevithick (1771-1833) who had insisted on using high pressure steam. Working in the Cornish tin-mining industry, he began ways to improve the existing low-powered steam engines of his day, primarily using this on stationary engines. He later applied what he called 'Strong Steam' to moveable engines, and tested these in London, Camborne and Ironbridge. Yet, it was at Penydarren near Merthyr Tydfil, that he began the railway revolution in 1804. His experiment was the result of a bet between two rival businessmen, who wagered over whether or not a machine could replace horses. Here the 1979-built replica of the locomotive that started it all, is seen at Railfest in its own enclosure.*

Top Right: *The 1804 engine was not a great success, as it was too heavy for the plateway on which it ran. Few people at the time gave the idea any chance of catching on; the fact that it did so is due to the industrialists of the time being forced into looking at machines to replace their horses during the critical years of the Napoleonic Wars, when fodder was both expensive and in short supply. On the Tuesday of Railfest the replica engine shed a wheel whilst being slowly demonstrated to the crowds; but it was an accident that would not have surprised Trevithick. It therefore provided a most unexpected demonstration of the kind of problems facing the early railway pioneers, and visitors could almost sense the atmosphere of 1804, when the real locomotive smashed the plateway on which it ran. Fortunately no-one was injured, although the engine driver will undoubtedly be able to tell the story for ever more.* David Tillotson

Bottom Right: *Whilst Railfest did not have W. C. Fields or Mae West, it did have a sense of the dramatic. Theatre interpretation, music and film were all part of Railfest and here, Platform 4 Theatre present 'Strong Steam'; even when the Penydarren locomotive wasn't able to be demonstrated, the show went on. The replica was however repaired and ran again by the end of the week, thanks to the fast work of skilled engineers on and off the site and the existence of a spare axle (not the kind of spare normally available to locomotives).* Tony Steadman

The Ffestiniog Railway in Yorkshire

The desire to re-create a little piece of Wales in Yorkshire saw the creation of a section of two-foot gauge line, to represent the narrow gauge industrial lines that sprang up all over Britain during the Victorian era. The Ffestiniog Railway were delighted to assist, and they built a new section of line to high standards on the museum site.

This was no small undertaking, but to ride behind the world's oldest operable narrow-gauge engine, in the world's oldest operational bogie coach, whilst passing by the brand new Virgin Pendolino set was one of the unique experiences available at Railfest.

Above: *Not since the late 1950s has a George England-built locomotive been within sight of the 'pedalling lion' or 'cat on a mangle' emblem on the side of a British Railways' locomotive. Here* Prince *is pictured alongside the Robinson 04, 2-8-0, a design which had been so vital to this nation during the troubled days of World War I. The use of the Robinson locomotives by the Railway Operating Department (ROD) is another of those examples of how the railways kept this country alive in two periods of world conflict. However, these 2-8-0s were not just good freight engines, but could also be seen on occasional passenger workings. This was demonstrated on the last day of Railfest, when 63601 ran the standard gauge service.* Tony Steadman

Top Right: *The unique sight of* Prince *and West Country Class* Blackmoor Vale *alongside each other. Not only is this a real contrast in liveries, as* Prince *in its 'Indian Red' paint scheme stands out against the 'Southern Sunshine' livery of Oliver Bullied's creation, but it is a juxtaposition that has never been seen before, nor is ever likely to be seen again. No doubt, some who witnessed the scene would have been reminded of that other standard gauge to narrow gauge railway interchange at Barnstaple. There the Southern Railway met the Lynton & Barnstaple's 1' 11½" gauge line, which had opened on May 11th 1898 and closed on 29th September 1935.*

Bottom Right: *Generations of children have grown up to the stories of* Thomas The Tank Engine *by the Reverend Wilbert Awdry, and these have gained their own unique place in the hearts and minds of readers and also their own unique place in 200 years of railway history. Of course, there are plenty of 'Thomas' events at preserved railways around the country, including the NRM, but some aspects of Railfest also created 'shades of Thomas'. The author frequently drew on real-life events and actual engines to create his stories. Therefore, following appearances in his books,* City of Truro *and* Prince (Duke *the Lost Engine) are shapes familiar to many people, but in neither fiction or fact had the two engines ever come together. Yet, at* Railfest Prince *and* City of Truro *finally met for the first time.*

OTHER GAUGES

Since the very early days of railways, people have had a desire to capture their favourite engines or scenes in miniature, thus giving birth to a massive and expanding hobby industry today.

To reflect this, Railfest paid tribute to the skills of scale modellers, particularly the live steam creations, which were to be seen hard at work entertaining visitors young and old during the celebrations.

Top Left: *York & District Model Engineers celebrating their 90th anniversary co-ordinated what must surely be one of the most intensively worked miniature railway operations ever held. The group managed to run steam on both tracks every day and carried about 14,000 people in the nine days.*

Bottom Left: *A diversion from the large steam exhibits, but nevertheless a historic locomotive in its own right, the 10¹/₄-inch-gauge* John Terence *of 1908 drew admiring looks from visitors and was kept busy throughout Railfest. For those who looked, the Stephenson Locomotive Society also had its historic 9¹/₂-inch gauge engine* Orion *on display, whilst Alan Keef Engineering showed the replica* Polar Bear *battery locomotive. Then there was the Nant Mawr and the Aberglaslyn Pass model in 16mm with live steam engines, which Trevithick would undoubtedly have marvelled at.*

SIGHTS AND SOUNDS

The whole concept of the event was to have a steady progression of experiences as you passed around the site, thus ensuring that there was more to see and do than the visitor first imagined. Indeed, so vibrant was the show, it was really difficult to take it all in during a single day. One group of American visitors, who were taking part in a 12-day tour of Britain's historic railways stated that even the two days allocated to visiting Railfest were simply 'too darn short'.

However long people stayed, there was much to see and do, from theatre presentations to track-laying demonstrations and from cab visits to the extensive trading area known as the Great Railway Bazaar.

Top Right: *Coaling and cleaning out engines and getting water to them was a daily chore on the site, and one that had to be completed before 10.00am. Here the Railfest project co-ordinator, Jon Pridmore, gets stuck into the task at around 07.30am, just two minutes after talking live on Radio York's morning drivetime programme.*

Bottom Right: *An historic fairground and the Great Railway Bazaar provided two diversions for those who needed an escape. The fairgrounds of Britain were once almost entirely steam-driven or used steam engines to generate electricity, so the link between these and Railfest was entirely appropriate.*

RAILFEST BY NIGHT

When long-standing NRM volunteer Tony Steadman offered to document Railfest for the NRM, the organisers were happy to agree; the NRM being a very busy place, not least because the event happened in the same year as the new museum at Shildon was scheduled to open.

Tony's photographs provide the backbone to this book, and this interlude demonstrates the results of his request to be allowed on the site at night. These evocative images were taken literally from 'dusk till dawn', with the cooperation of the NRM's Security Team, at a time when Railfest staff and volunteers had 'knocked off' for a well-earned rest.

Left: *As though it has just drifted in on an overnight train like the Night Ferry,* Blackmoor Vale *oozes magic in the still light of the evening.* All images by Tony Steadman

Top Right: *As night falls,* Electra *gleams under the lights whilst* Yvonne *drifts steam. The EM2 (Class 77)* Electra *represents Britain's first attempt at main line electrification using 1500v DC overhead equipment on its Manchester to Sheffield and Wath route. Although planned prior to World War II, the route via Woodhead finally opened in 1954 and half a century later the locomotive was presented at Railfest as it would have been on the opening day. When the route ceased to carry passenger traffic, E27000 was sold to Dutch State Railways in 1968. It remained in use in the Netherlands until 1986, before being brought back for preservation in the UK.*

Centre Right: *Resting ready for another day the 1903-built GWR 4-4-0* City of Truro *gleams under the lights as dusk falls on Railfest. The photographer has captured here a timeless scene and gives the impression that he could have been at work a century ago.*

Bottom Right: *Like a silver bullet, the Advanced Passenger Train (Experimental) gleams in the artificial light, having been re-painted just prior to Railfest and ready for a new starring role in the NRM's new Locomotion museum at Shildon.*

RAILFEST: WHEN THE SHOW WAS OVER

Once Railfest closed its doors to the public, the NRM and the volunteer groups still had a massive amount of work to do, especially as arrangements had to be put in place to return all the exhibits to their usual homes. Some exhibits had to leave early in order to meet other commitments, but after nine days the site was still packed. Now the reverse of the unloading operation had to be undertaken, as friends old and new said goodbye!

Above: *Unique sights were available to the team of NRM staff and volunteers who worked to prepare the Railfest site and those who helped with the clear-up afterwards. Here the Siemens E4 (built 1909) from the Stephenson Railway Museum on Tyneside meets the Beattie well tank (built 1874), which is usually shedded at Bodmin in Cornwall. This meeting of two engines from opposite ends of the country also brings together another coincidental link, as Trevithick's home county was Cornwall, whilst George Stephenson began his railway career on Tyneside.*

Top Right: *Although this Class 37 provided by EWS was not part of the show, these robust survivors from the steam era are now historic locomotives in their own right. The English Electric-built engine, with its original nose doors welded shut, is seen here as it arrives to assist with the shunting operations at the close of Railfest. In its everyday working clothes, 37057 prepares to move the smartly adorned Class 47* Prince William. *Presented to the NRM on 4th June 2004, 47798 (the former Royal Train engine) is one of the long-lived Class 47 diesels, and is one that has had no less than four numbers and two names during its working life. Like the 37s, the 47s have played an integral part in both passenger and freight operations since the Modernisation Plan of the 1950s led to their introduction.*

Bottom Right: *Many of the earlier pioneering diesel classes, which were introduced in the BR Modernisation Plan have long since passed out of service. However, as seen above the Class 37s, and 47s still soldier on at the time of writing. Another surviving class is the English Electric (Class 08) shunting engine. Here we see the NRM's very own example, 08911 as it makes quite a contrast with the superbly finished Deltic D9009. Although the 08 is in need of a coat of paint, it was in fact donated to the museum just before Railfest. It certainly came in useful to assist with the moves before, during and after the event and is seen here whilst transferring* Alycidon *to temporary display in the Great Hall.*

Top Left: *Last minute visitors to Railfest were able to get a rare view 'under the covers' of the nine-car Pendolino as it prepares to move. Alongside is the Alstom engineer who had managed to keep the lights on for the nine days of Railfest using a generator the size of a truck; no mean task as the original calculations were for a seven-car Pendolino.*

Bottom Left: *Here we say farewell to the 15" gauge engines* Smoky Joe *and* Sutton Belle *after nine days of solid work. The Cleethorpes Coast Light Railway team worked the 15" gauge line with colleagues from the Rhyl Lakeside Railway, the Sherwood Forest Railway and individuals who had travelled from Oxfordshire to Cumbria and points in between to help at the show; between them they ensured that the 'Minimum Gauge' story was not lost in the celebrations.*

Bottom Right: *After it was all over there were of course the memories of sights and sounds, many of which this book recalls. There were other tangible reminders, not least the new and very easy walking access between the NRM and York station, which was opened on Saturday 29th May 2004. There was also a brand new rail arena for the museum, which will form a useful facility for exhibitions in future years, whatever form these take. There were also some very tired staff and volunteers, but to balance this many happy visitors. The celebration of two hundred years of steam and railways had left its mark in more ways than one.* Tony Steadman

CONCLUSION

Twenty-four years after the 'Rocket 150' celebrations and ten years after rail privatisation, Railfest proved that Britain's railways are loved as much today as they were when they first started, and that with investment their future can be just as interesting as their past.

Railfest also enabled the National Railway Museum to reinforce its position at the centre of the railway stage, as its 70,000 visitors will no doubt testify. It left behind the physical legacy of a site that is a splendid and proven arena for rail, along with a direct link from York station to the NRM.

Above: *Dogs of war? Here Riddles Austerity 2-10-0* Dame Vera Lynn *meets the Southern Railway Q1 0-6-0 (C1/33001), which was specially returned to York for the event. Both were very impressed by Railfest, but will they ever meet again?*

Many, many companies and individuals contributed to the success of Railfest, from big players in the rail industry to the individual volunteers who gave time to host visitors around the site, and this book is a tribute to their efforts and success.

Here's to the future of rail, from pleasure lines to those using the very latest technology; they all have a part to play in a developing and ever fascinating story!

Roy Wilson from the Guild of Railway Artists demonstrates how to capture an image without a wide-angle lens. Simon Townsend